HEALING HEALTH

AND WHOLENESS

First published in Great Britain for

Life Changing Ministries
Bemersley House
Gitana Street
Hanley
Stoke-on-Trent
ST1 1DY

By Ian Matthews Associates and Verité CM Ltd

ISBN: The catalogue record for this book is available from the
British Library

Produced by Ian Matthews Associates, Shrewsbury.
www.im-associates.co.uk

Typesetting and design by Verité CM Ltd., Worthing.
www.veritecm.com

Printed and bound in Great Britain by
Antony Rowe Ltd., Chippenham, Wiltshire

CONTENTS

INTRODUCTION

There are many books today on the subject of healing which deal with different aspects of this immense topic. I do not want you to think that I have all of the answers on healing because I do not. I have had a quest throughout the years of ministering to hurting people to simply help them as much as I can. Over the years I have learned many things that will probably benefit others.

I have waited several years before writing this book, since I am still learning and will go on learning until Jesus returns. I trust that you are still open to learn, which is probably the reason you are reading this book!

May I challenge you to search the Scriptures before making any final conclusions. Also, make sure that you have a revelation in your own heart before acting in faith for your healing. You cannot depend upon someone else's revelation of healing. You have to get it for yourself! I pray that the penny will drop for you as you study this book and healing, health and wholeness will be a reality for you and your loved ones and also those to whom The Lord calls you to minister.

CHAPTER 1

HEALING FOR THE WHOLE MAN

I was 19 years old when I became a born again Christian. I had a very dramatic conversion after leading a very worldly life. During my teens I developed a problem with headaches which were so severe that they would stay for about two days before any relief. Anyway, after being saved for three weeks I was invited to attend a conference where The Word of God was preached and healing was practised. During one of the meetings the preacher stood up and asked those who suffer with headaches to stand up. I shot up off my seat along with many others and the man prayed for us to be healed. I was healed from that day and never had a headache like those in over 23 years. I knew then that healing was real.

This prompted a desire in me to find out all I could about healing and so I studied the Word of God very closely and made some wonderful discoveries. The Word of God has many references to healing that you are probably familiar with. However, I am going to assume that you know nothing since you may have only just become a Christian! Here are a few references taken from the whole Bible.

> *But unto you that fear my name shall the Sun of righteousness arise with healing in his wings; and ye shall go forth, and grow up as calves of the stall.*
>
> Mal 4:2

> *And Jesus went about all the cities and villages, teaching in their synagogues, and preaching the gospel of the kingdom, and healing every sickness and every disease among the people.*
>
> Matt 9:35

CHAPTER 1   *Healing for the Whole Man*

And said, "If thou wilt diligently hearken to the voice of the LORD thy God, and wilt do that which is right in his sight, and will give ear to his commandments, and keep all his statutes, I will put none of these diseases upon thee, which I have brought upon the Egyptians: for I am the LORD that healeth thee."

Exod 15:26

Who forgiveth all thine iniquities; who healeth all thy diseases;

Ps 103:3

He healeth the broken in heart, and bindeth up their wounds.

Ps 147:3

O LORD my God, I cried unto thee, and thou hast healed me.

Ps 30:2

What does it mean then to be healed? Is it just healing from physical ailments? Let us examine this in some detail. According to Strong's Dictionary one of the words for healing means;

7495 rapha' (raw-faw'); or raphah (raw-faw'); a primitive root; properly, to mend (by stitching), i.e. (figuratively) to cure: KJV — cure, (cause to) heal, physician, repair, X thoroughly, make whole. This is where the familiar phrase 'Jehova Rapha' comes from; the Lord our healer. This suggests that healing is a complete thing for the whole man. In fact, when you study the Word of

God closely you will find that healing is for every aspect of the human being, body, soul and spirit.

> Beloved, **I wish above all things that thou mayest prosper and be in health, even as thy soul prospereth.**
>
> 3 Jn 1:2

> And Jesus went about all Galilee, teaching in their synagogues, and preaching the gospel of the kingdom, **and healing all manner of sickness and all manner of disease among the people.**
>
> Matt 4:23

> And his fame went throughout all Syria: **and they brought unto him all sick people that were taken with divers diseases and torments, and those which were possessed with devils, and those which were lunatick, and those that had the palsy; and he healed them.**
>
> Matt 4:24

These three verses cover most of the problems that people get, including mental, physical, emotional and all kinds of tormenting illness. In fact, the word 'salvation' means wholeness for body, soul and spirit. What usually happens when people read a book like this is *they have lots of questions*!

Hopefully, all of your questions will be answered as you read through each chapter. Don't miss anything out! Read it all.

Healing in the atonement.

This simply means that when Jesus died on the cross that not only did He pay the price for sin but also sickness and disease.

> Surely he hath borne our **griefs**, and carried our **sorrows**: yet we did esteem him stricken, smitten of God, and afflicted.
>
> Isa 53:4

> But he was wounded for our transgressions, he was bruised for our iniquities: the chastisement of our peace was upon him; and with his stripes we are healed.
>
> Isa 53:5

Let us look at the 2 words that I have put in bold.

1. Griefs. Strongs Dictionary says this

2483 choliy (khol-ee'); from 2470; **malady, anxiety, calamity**: KJV — disease, grief, sick (-ness).

That means that Jesus actually bore all my disease, grief, sickness, anxiety, malady and calamities when He hung upon the cross! Hallelujah! That is good news. All I have to do is to believe it!

2. Sorrows.

This is very similar and means; **pain, grief and sorrow.**

No wonder Is 53:5 says that *we are healed.* It is obvious that if Jesus Christ has already paid the price for my healing 2000 years ago then I must be healed! No wonder Jesus cried out when He was on the cross, IT IS FINISHED! Not only was He paying the price for our sin but also our healing. In fact, He also paid the price for our poverty. So you can be healed financially also!

> **For ye know the grace of our Lord Jesus Christ, that, though he was rich, yet for your sakes he became poor, that ye through his poverty might be rich.**
>
> 2 Cor 8:9

Jesus did this upon the cross. He was not poor in His earthly walk at all. Jews were not poor then and they are not poor today either! Look at the following verse!

> *And they crucified him,* ***and parted his garments, casting lots:*** *that it might be fulfilled which was spoken by the prophet,* ***They parted my garments among them, and upon my vesture did they cast lots.***
>
> Matt 27:35

When was the last time that you heard of someone casting lots over a poor man for his old clothes? Old clothes from a poor person are usually taken to the charity shop! It seems obvious that the clothes that Jesus was wearing were very costly and so much so that wealthy Roman soldiers were fighting for them after His death.

You see, Jesus was not poor during His life at all. He did walk in miracles when He needed some money; the mouth of the fish to pay His taxes for instance.

But when He was on the cross He became poor on the cross to bear our poverty so that we could prosper just like the Jews; in fact, more so. Read Romans 9,10 and 11 sometime. It says that we gentiles should make the Jews jealous to provoke them to come to Jesus!

Thus, when Jesus was on the cross He did all of this;

1. He took our sins to make us righteous. 2 Cor 5:21.

2. He took our sickness so that we could be healed. Matt 8:17.

3. He took our poverty to make us rich. 2 Cor 8:9. (You may also wish to order a copy of our book entitled 'What the Bible says about Your Provision and Prosperity', the address is at the end of this book).

4. He took all our defeat and gave us victory. Rom 8:35-37.

5. He took all the negative things in life and gave us positive things instead!

> *To appoint unto them that mourn in Zion, to give unto them beauty for ashes, the oil of joy for mourning, the garment of praise for the spirit of heaviness; that they might be called trees of righteousness, the planting of the LORD, that he might be glorified.*
>
> Is 01.3

CHAPTER 2

HOW TO RECEIVE HEALING FOR YOURSELF

Many Christians have a preconceived idea about how they can be healed. Unfortunately, this is the fault of the church in general by putting too much emphasis on the laying on of hands for healing. I want to make a statement at the very start here. Healing is available for every believer, at any time of the day or night, right where we are. We simply need some teaching as to how to RECEIVE IT. It is not enough to tell you that healing is available. We need to know how to release it.

Firstly, we need to be convinced that it is the will of God to heal us. Let us deal with this to start with. Consider salvation. The Word of God declares that it is the will of God for all to be saved, does it not?

> ***Who will have all men to be saved***, *and to come unto the knowledge of the truth.*
>
> 1 Tim 2:4

> *The Lord is not slack concerning his promise, as some men count slackness; but is longsuffering toward us,* ***not willing that any should perish, but that all should come to repentance.***
>
> 2 Pet 3:9

However, millions of people are going to hell without the knowledge of Jesus Christ as Lord and Saviour. Thus, it is the will of God for them to be saved and Jesus has done everything that he can to make salvation possible but man still has to accept it for himself. It is the same with healing. Healing is available for all but not everyone knows how to receive it.

CHAPTER 2   *How to Receive Healing for Yourself*

> *My people are destroyed for lack of knowledge: because thou hast rejected knowledge, I will also reject thee, that thou shalt be no priest to me; seeing thou hast forgotten the law of thy God, I will also forget thy children.*
>
> Hosea 4:6

Therefore we need some knowledge to help us to receive our healing.

I trust that the following points will help you to understand that it is God's will to heal you.

1. God sent His Word and healed you.

> **He sent his word, and healed them, and delivered them from their destructions.**
>
> Ps 107:20

2. Jesus never laid His hands on people and made them sick. No; He healed them.

3. He made atonement for all sickness and disease on the cross.

4. Several of the spiritual gifts are given for our healing. 1 Cor 12:8-10

> *Praise God; now we can find out how to appropriate this healing for ourselves. I am going to tell you how I go about claiming my healing which I have been doing now for 22 years.*

1. I rebuke the sickness, pain or virus in the name of Jesus Christ and command it to go!

> *Behold, I give unto you power to tread on serpents and scorpions, and over all the power of the enemy: and nothing shall by any means hurt you.*
>
> Luke 10:19

> *Submit yourselves therefore to God. Resist the devil, and he will flee from you.*
>
> James 4:7

2. Then I speak the Word of God over my body and I confess His Word.

> *But he was wounded for our transgressions, he was bruised for our iniquities: the chastisement of our peace was upon him; **and with his stripes we are healed.***
>
> Isa 53:5

> *Who his own self bare our sins in his own body on the tree, that we, being dead to sins, should live unto righteousness: **by whose stripes ye were healed.***
>
> 1 Pet 2:24

> *Who forgiveth all thine iniquities; who **healeth all thy diseases;***
>
> Ps 103:3

3. I then rejoice in God for healing me by faith even though there may or may not be any improvement. We walk by faith and not by sight.

> *(As it is written, I have made thee a father of many nations,) before him whom he believed,*

*even God, who quickeneth the dead, **and calleth those things which be not as though they were.***

Rom 4:17

While we look not at the things which are seen, but at the things which are not seen: for the things which are seen are temporal; but the things which are not seen are eternal.

2 Cor 4:18

You see, sickness is subject to change but the Word of God is not subject to change. Therefore, my faith is based on the rock solid Word of God and not on what my body tells me. This is how faith works. I have lived this way for 22 years and it keeps working. If it doesn't work then the problem is not with God! It must be with me. God is totally consistent all the time and never changes. Let me share a couple of instances where I was wrong.

The Lord spoke to me one time about doing something in our church in Salford. I was too proud to do it for fear of what people would say. God told me to dance in church publicly and to lead the church into dancing in worship. For 2 years I rebelled against this word. Then, I noticed a problem developing with my right hand. An open sore appeared which was very painful. I rebuked it as usual and confessed the Word of God. I did everything right according to God's Word, but it grew worse. I went to a conference where I was alone with God in my room. I spent a few hours in prayer and was asking The Lord why it would not heal. God said this to me. 'You are in rebellion'. I said, 'Me Lord? Never!' He then told me that I had rebelled against His Word regarding dancing in church. I repented and then within 5 days I was totally healed after 6 months of needless pain. I have never had anything like that since. That was 13 years ago. Thus, rebellion against God can bring on sickness and disease. We need to humble ourselves and ask Him if there is anything that we need to put right that he has told us to do.

The second thing that I trust will help some people is a very recent thing. I have been flying all over the world for the last 7 years. I have travelled to 52 countries on around 850 different flights. The base of my spine started to give me a sharp pain during year 2000. I used my faith and rebuked the devil. I stood on the Word of God for my healing. It grew worse. I then asked The Lord what was wrong. He told me that it was my unbelief! I said, 'In what way was I in unbelief?' The Lord then told me that my unbelief was by not using my faith to believe God for Business Class and First Class flights! I had looked many a time at the price of flying in Business and First Class and it is so expensive; sometimes up to 7 times more than Economy Class. For instance, a flight to Los Angeles costs about £400 in Economy. The same journey on the same plane in Business Class costs £2500. First Class is about £5000. You see what I mean?

So, with all the flying that I do my annual travelling bill was going to jump from about £7000 per year to about £25,000 per year. I took a big gulp and repented of unbelief in not taking the step sooner. I then vowed to God that I would not travel in Economy Class again for long haul flights. I am about to go to the USA in 2 weeks time for the 16th. time and I am going across the Atlantic in Business Class in a big leather chair. Then in the USA many of my internal flights are in First Class. My back is about 85 percent healed. When I booked my tickets this time for the flights I only had about £900 to spend on the flights. The total fare cost £3239. All the money came in in about 10 days from the moment that I booked the tickets by faith. Our God is an awesome God. Obedience is so important.

> *If ye be willing and obedient, ye shall eat*
> *the good of the land:*
>
> Isa 1:19

CHAPTER 3

HOW TO STAY HEALTHY
AND KEEP YOUR HEALING

For those of you who are already in good health it is important to speak the Word of God concerning your healing and health on a regular basis. This builds up a strong fortress against the attacks of the enemy. I speak health over my whole body regularly by praising God for my healing. Here is a sample prayer which you can adapt for your own life.

'Father, I thank you that Your Word has promised me health for my entire being, body, soul and spirit. By Your stripes I am healed and I was healed 2000 years ago in The Wonderful Name of Jesus Christ. I am walking in health even as my soul is prospering and I thank you that I am protected from all the attacks of the enemy. I refuse any aches, pains, viruses or any kind of infirmity in my body and I praise You Lord that I remain in the best of health to serve You all the days of my life. Amen!'

There are also practical things that we can do to stay healthy which is very important. The Word of God says:

> *What? know ye not that your body is the temple of the Holy Ghost which is in you, which ye have of God, and ye are not your own?*
>
> 1 Cor 6:19

Thus we need to look after our bodies as well and not abuse them through neglect.

> *For bodily exercise profiteth little: but godliness is profitable unto all things, having promise of the life that now is, and of that which is to come.*
>
> 1 Tim 4:8

This verse tells us that living a Godly life is more important than simply physical exercise. However, it does not say that we should not have any exercise! The word 'little' in this verse means 'for a short time' or 'for a season'. In other words, some exercise is important but leading a life of purity and holiness is far more important, both for this life and the one to come. Physical exercise helps to keep the oxygen flowing through our body since the blood flows faster with some exercise.

We are living in an age where the car has taken over most of our lives. I am as guilty as the next. It is so easy to jump into the car to go to the corner shop than it is to walk. After all it is quicker! We have all done it for the sake of saving time. In Bible days they had no cars, buses, planes or motor vehicles of any description. They either caught the camel or walked! Jesus talks a lot about walking everywhere He goes!It is amazing how unfit we become by not taking a little exercise. We all need to take some each week. My wife goes swimming once or twice a week, which she enjoys. I don't like swimming and so I go and play golf. Some say that it is a long walk spoiled but I really enjoy it. It helps me to switch off from all the things I have to think about in ministry. You have to when playing golf or else that little ball will not go where it is supposed to! You may think that this is a carnal pursuit but it gets me walking about 4 miles each week, which works for me. Some people like to go into the hills and walk.

Whatever is best for you, do it and keep the oxygen flowing around your body. I am told that walking is one of the best forms of exercise which we can do all through life.

Why not try it for yourself for a few weeks and just see how unfit you are when you reach a hill! However, when you do it regularly you start to feel the benefit. This is a good habit to form for all of us!

Food

You knew that this one would be coming next, didn't you? Don't go to the next chapter. Read on!

I am not an expert on food, nutrition, blood groups or any specialist field. However, I do know that eating the wrong foods will affect our performance and could lead to health problems. The world is constantly telling us to watch what we eat. It is about time we Christians did the same!

One thing I do know and that is we are all different. Some people can eat seemingly what they want to and never put on weight. Others eat carefully and seem to just bloom! Someone told me recently that our blood group makes a big difference as to what we can eat. I am not qualified to go into any detail but it is certainly worth finding out. I believe that we all need to be led by the Holy Spirit as to what is good for us and what is not. Doughnuts are not good for any of us! Fizzy drinks can be really harmful in large doses. I remember visiting a minister friend one time and he ate chips every day and had loads of fresh cream. Before he was 50 he had to have a triple heart by-pass. I have another friend who used to pastor and he was always eating burgers and fast food. He was overweight and did not seem to care. When he was 50 he had a heart attack. I am talking about Godly, Spirit filled believers! We need to watch what we eat. Many claim that organic foods are better for us because most of the food that we buy has been treated with potentially harmful chemicals. Find out for yourself what works for you. A little bit of research could save you from health problems in later life.

I know that as I grew older I did not need as much food as I used to when I was young. Until I was 28 years old I could eat 3 good meals a day apart from when I was fasting. However, when I was 28 my body started to change. I noticed that my stomach began to grow. So I started to reduce the amount of food that I ate. I eat far less than I used to since my body does not need it. I have the sort of metabolism that needs regular attention. I have to be careful what I eat all the time now.

God has given me the responsibility to look after my body as well as my spiritual life. Many Christians eat to comfort themselves. Gluttony is a sin.

> *For the drunkard and the glutton shall come*
> *to poverty: and drowsiness shall clothe a*
> *man with rags.*
>   Prov 23:21

> *And put a knife to thy throat, if thou be a*
> *man given to appetite.*
>   Prov 23:2

Overeating causes a lust of the flesh to keep eating more. Some people need deliverance from a spirit of gluttony. Some simply need to discipline their flesh life and constantly monitor what they are eating. What about you?

CHAPTER 4

MAN'S EXPERIENCE VERSUS THE WORD OF GOD

I have been challenged many times regarding healing since many have 'tried' to pray for their healing and it has not manifested. Many have had tragic situations in their lives which causes questions. I have heard many people say 'What about Johnny, he prayed for healing and was never healed'. How do we answer such a question? My quest is to learn all that I can about healing and help as many as I can. If we base our belief on other people's experience, which is contrary to God's Word, then we must seek God to find the answer. One person was heard to say about this subject, 'We don't know enough'.

In other words, if healing has not manifested yet then maybe we need to learn more about it. This is true in my life. I have learned not to question God but to trust Him and believe His Word. He is right and I am learning the humble way to treat this subject. We have all had experiences that don't come absolutely in line with what God says in His Word, but that is no reason to build a theology of your own by saying that God does not always heal. The fact of the matter is that we did not know enough at the time. Our faith in The Word of God should not be shaken by experience which produces unbelief but rather a strong desire to learn more and have victory the next time! God's Word remains the same. We do not change it because our experience is different from it! This may sound harsh to some of you and even be a slap in the face but I pray and trust that it will peel back the unbelief that has built up in your life and that a simple faith in God will bring you into victory.

I want to share a testimony from my own ministry that will always live with me until Jesus comes back. I was a pastor in Salford, Manchester. I had just taken over and was getting to know the new people. I was introduced to a precious lady called Mabel. She told me about her illness. She had sugar diabetes of an extreme kind and had to pump an enormous amount of insulin into her body every day. She was a Christian who loved God very much. I went through the Scriptures with her regarding healing and she said that she believed God's Word about healing but that she was still very sick. I told her to receive her healing and to start to confess it out loud each day. She became angry with me and told me that she was still sick. I told her that God said that she was healed 2000 years ago. She said, 'That's right, but I am still sick'. This went on for many months. I visited her in the hospital and told her the same thing. I was teaching her to believe God's Word for her healing. She would get angry at me and said, 'I know God's Word says that by the stripes of Jesus I was healed, but I am still sick!' I was very patient with her and kept praying for her to receive a revelation of faith for healing. One day she phoned me up and shouted down the telephone, 'I am healed, I am healed!' I hardly needed the telephone she was shouting so loudly. I said, 'What has happened to you?' She said, 'I've got it. God said it and I believe it. I am healed.'

Now, nothing had changed in her body until that time. She was still taking the full measure of insulin. However, I knew that diabetes could no longer stay in her body, now that she had a revelation of God's Word on healing. She started praising God for her healing and from the moment that she had the revelation her body started to change in line with her faith. The doctor could not understand what was happening to her. He had to keep reducing her insulin amounts each day for about 3 weeks until she did not need any more. Her blood sugar was perfectly normal! She was healed in the natural and went and got a job! Hallelujah!

The problem was that she had been under the teaching that God heals some but not everybody. This produced unbelief which had to be confronted with the Word of God every day for 6 months until faith ignited in her. The miracle power of God was released immediately when Mabel believed the Word of God. I have spoken to her recently after 13 years and she is still well. Praise God for evermore.We need to confess the Word of God concerning healing on a regular basis which produces this kind of faith. My faith is very strong now after doing this daily for 22 years. I know that I am healed and I refuse any symptoms of sickness and disease. It does not belong to me. Healing is mine by right. It has already been paid for on my behalf. My job is to stay in faith all the days of my life and fulfil my destiny on this earth! My experience now is based on the Word of God. My body is now in line with what God says.I must tell you what happened recently. My wife, Ruth told me that we had all been asked to go and have a medical check-up at the new doctors. I had not seen a doctor for over 20 years. Ruth had only seen doctors through having babies. We simply believed the Word of God. Our children have hardly had a day off school all through life and enjoy splendid health.

We arrived in the nurse's office and she gave all four Newports a thorough examination. Joy was first (our daughter).The nurse said that she was boring! Joy was so healthy. Then David; the same thing. The nurse said he was so healthy. She seemed determined to find something wrong with one of us. Then Ruth went through and the nurse was amazed that all of us were so healthy. Then I went in and she gave me the full works. She examined me and then said to me, 'What is your secret? I have never seen a whole family in such perfect health'. I was able to witness to her and almost saw her saved. She was so impressed. When we left she said, 'I don't suppose that I will see you for another 20 years, will I?' I said, 'No,' and went on my way thanking and praising God for His goodness to us as a family.

CHAPTER 5

COMMON SENSE!

When a person becomes a Christian it seems that many have the wrong idea that common sense is foolishness. Many think that we can live the way that we want to and do anything and it won't affect our health. How naive can we be!

God has given us basic wisdom that says, 'If you lift a bag of potatoes that is too heavy then you could hurt your back'. It is wrong to think that we cannot injure ourselves physically by doing what our body was not designed to do. It is common sense to put on warmer clothing in the winter or else we can catch a natural cold. Some think that we can forget such principles and God will heal us anyway. I don't think so. We should use common sense at all times to prevent such things from happening. Some of us have had to repent more than once for abusing our body before God can heal us. Healing is still available, even if you have done something very silly and damaged your body. You still have a right to claim Divine healing after you have repented, but it would have been easier if we had not acted unwisely in the first place!My mum taught me so many good things about common sense and I wish that I had taken her advice more when I was younger! I can almost hear some of you saying, 'Amen'.

Some people have abused their bodies in other ways also. 'Workaholism' can creep up on us Christians and can lead to stress etc and bring on all kinds of problems. Our body was only meant to cope with a certain amount of work. If you have any signs that you are overworking, then listen to the natural voice of your body and do something about it before it gets worse. It is amazing how your body will tell you when things are not right. I remember years ago that I was working far too hard as a pastor and I developed stress pains across my chest. It was a symptom of overwork and so I disciplined myself to take a day off each week and stopped working for God. I learned how to work with God instead. I was trying to do the work of the Holy Spirit instead of being a servant and only doing what I was called upon to do. Many of us in ministry have been caught in the same trap. We try so hard to please God sometimes and if something is not working we increase the workload to see if that will work.

> *I am the vine, ye are the branches: He that abideth in me, and I in him, the same bringeth forth much fruit: for without me ye can do nothing.*   John 15:5

Only what God tells us to do will bear any fruit. The work that we do in our own strength will produce nothing anyway, so stop what you are doing and seek His face until He speaks to you and then have the courage to act on what He says. That is how ministry works. In my life I seek to do only commanded work. I don't want to preach my own sermons, only what Father has given me. I don't want to write a single word of a book unless it is inspired by The Lord; I don't want to fly off to another country unless God is with me, because I cannot do anything without Him! Take a look at these verses:

> *Behold, in this thou art not just: I will answer thee, that **God is greater than man.***
> Job 33:12

Why dost thou strive against him? For he giveth not account of any of his matters.

Job 33:13

For God speaketh once, yea twice, yet man perceiveth it not.

Job 33:14

In a dream, in a vision of the night, when deep sleep falleth upon men, in slumberings upon the bed;

Job 33:15

Then he openeth the ears of men, and sealeth their instruction,

Job 33:16

That he may withdraw man from his purpose, and hide pride from man.

Job 33:17

I pray that all of your self-conceived ideas and purposes of man will fail quickly and you will find a Word from God that will bring you up to higher ground and begin to walk in your true destiny. Make a decision today to stop working for God and begin to work with Him. I cannot emphasise this point enough.

CHAPTER 6

MAINTAINING A CONSISTENT CONFESSION

Take a close look at the following Scriptures:

> *Seeing then that we have a great high priest, that is passed into the heavens, Jesus the Son of God, **let us hold fast our profession.***
>
> Heb 4:14

> *For we have not an high priest which cannot be touched with the feeling of our infirmities; but was in all points tempted like as we are, yet without sin.*
>
> Heb 4:15

> *Let us therefore come boldly unto the throne of grace, that we may obtain mercy, and find grace to help in time of need.*
>
> Heb 4:16

> ***Let us hold fast the profession of our faith without wavering; (for he is faithful that promised).***
>
> Heb 10:23

There is great power in consistency and especially when it comes to faith.

Since the day I was saved I have never doubted for one minute my salvation, no matter how I was feeling. That is being consistent in faith. The same is now true for healing for me after an initial struggle to overcome in that area. Once I had the revelation that healing was just as much a part of my covenant as salvation, nothing would shift me from my confession. I was healed and that was it. However, I have had to fight off the devil's attacks over the years and I have always won. Glory to God! Just because you have revelation of healing does not mean that you will not be challenged from time to time. This only makes me stronger. You can't have a victory without a battle!

Now, it is not only important to maintain a positive confession of healing but also we should be careful not to speak negative things about ourselves. That brings contradiction. What do I mean by that? For instance, some people go through life saying things like; 'I am afraid it is going to rain today', 'I fear that I have missed the train' and such like. Allowing fear in your vocabulary is a bad habit that needs to be broken; also, things like death. 'I am dead certain about that!' 'I am dying to go to the shops'. Look at what God's Word says:

> **Death and life are in the power of the tongue: and they that love it shall eat the fruit thereof.**
>
> Prov 18:21

> *And Jesus answering saith unto them, 'Have faith in God.'*
>
> Mark 11:22

> *For verily I say unto you,* **That whosoever shall say unto this mountain, Be thou removed, and be thou cast into the sea; and shall not doubt in his heart, but shall believe that those things which he saith shall come to pass; he shall have whatsoever he saith.**
>
> Mark 11:23

Therefore I say unto you, What things soever ye desire, when ye pray, believe that ye receive them, and ye shall have them.

Mark 11:24

Therefore, we need to watch carefully what we say about anything and everything. I never speak sickness, disease, aches, pains, lack, poverty, can't afford, depression, sadness, misery or anything to agree with the devil. I speak victory, healing, prosperity, joy, gladness, destiny, and everything that is positive. Look at the life of Jesus and examine the words that He spoke all the time. He was very careful about what He said at all times. His words were full of power, purpose, destiny, healing etc. If you are not aware what comes out of your mouth then get a voice activated tape recorder and listen to yourself talk all day and see how much negative rubbish comes out of your life. Agree with God's Word and lead a consistent life of victory every day and just see what happens just by changing your confession. It works!

CHAPTER 7

THE WILL OF GOD AND HEALING

I believe that this will help some people, because I know many friends who have found themselves out of the will of God for their life and had problems with their health. I know a pastor in my own city who was pastoring and developed a serious illness. It transpired that God had been speaking to him about doing a new ministry which he was resisting. As soon as he obeyed the next step for his life the healing power of God became a reality. You see when we are out of God's will it is a form of rebellion called disobedience. This gives the devil a legal opportunity to attack us. Our protection mechanism has been compromised and he can have a field day with us.

> *And the Lord said, 'Simon, Simon, behold, Satan hath desired to have you, that he may sift you as wheat:'*
>
> Luke 22:31

> *But I have prayed for thee, that thy faith fail not: and when thou art converted, strengthen thy brethren.*
>
> Luke 22:32

Have you ever tried to operate in faith and found that you were getting nowhere? It is often because we are out of His perfect will. If you are struggling in your health then ask God now if you have obeyed Him thoroughly. As you simply and humbly obey Him then your healing will manifest soon afterwards.

How can we know the will of God then? The secret is peace. Do you have peace in your heart where you are now? Has God given you any direction for your life to make any changes? If not then you are in the will of God. If you know that the will of God is changing in your heart then the best thing to do is fast and pray. This will tune your spirit in with the Holy Spirit so that you can hear His voice more accurately. That is what I do and have been doing for 21 years. There is no substitute for fasting and praying in the Spirit. Also, if you think that God has spoken to you about the next step then He will confirm it to you in many ways so that you are left with no doubt.Since we have mentioned fasting at this point I will tell you something else of vital importance to anyone who is suffering from any kind of illness.

Read these verses:

Is it such a fast that I have chosen? a day for a man to afflict his soul? is it to bow down his head as a bulrush, and to spread sackcloth and ashes under him? wilt thou call this a fast, and an acceptable day to the LORD?

Isa 58:5

Is not this the fast that I have chosen? to loose the bands of wickedness, to undo the heavy burdens, and to let the oppressed go free, and that ye break every yoke?

Isa 58:6

Is it not to deal thy bread to the hungry, and that thou bring the poor that are cast out to thy house? When thou seest the naked, that thou cover him; and that thou hide not thyself from thine own flesh?

Isa 58:7

> *Then shall thy light break forth as the morning, and **thine health shall spring forth speedily:** and thy righteousness shall go before thee; the glory of the LORD shall be thy reward.*
>
> Isa 58:8

Thus through fasting our healing can manifest.

I had a situation a couple of years ago where I had a pain in my side. I rebuked it and did everything that I knew. It did not shift. It kept on giving me pain for about six months. I had been confessing God's Word and praising God for my healing.

I asked the Lord what else I needed to do and He told me to go on a long fast. I agreed to do a 21 day fast in preparation for my 40th year and also for my own healing. It was great fast; one of the easiest I have ever done as well as the longest. However, the pain was still in my side until day 17 of the fast. On the seventeenth day it just healed up and I have never had it since! Praise God! My health did spring forth speedily. Also, I have had a much greater anointing in the area of healing when praying for people. I have seen some of the most powerful healings and miracles since that fast. It was certainly God's chosen fast.

Throughout the 20 years I have been in ministry I have always taken about two to three days a week to fast, for the first 14 years or so anyway. Now that I travel so much I take a few long fasts throughout the year, which keeps me sensitive to His voice.

If that is speaking to you then you have nothing to lose, apart from a few pounds in weight! I have just been on a seven day fast and I lost eleven pounds in weight. Always drink plenty of liquids during a fast. I find myself drinking about twice as much as normal. I drink water, juice, tea, coffee, Oxo cubes (crushed into boiling water, of course!). I find that it does not make any difference what I am drinking; it is the withdrawal from food that is the most important thing about fasting. If you just drink water then that's okay; do what works for you. It is good to pray in the spirit when you fast, either during the fast or straight afterwards. I used to pray all through the fast but I was always so tired. I think the Holy Spirit prompted me to do my praying after I had started eating, since I then had strength to pray. Do what works for you.

I know that some people say that fasting any longer than three days is unbelief, but I notice that in the Bible there were many times when fasting was practised for much longer than three days. Moses did 40 days. Jesus did 40 days. Paul did 14 days etc.

Do what God tells you to do and we shall all be happy!

CHAPTER 8

ASKING OTHERS TO PRAY FOR YOU

What does the Bible say about asking someone else to pray for you?

> *Again I say unto you,* **that if two of you shall agree on earth as touching any thing that they shall ask, it shall be done for them of my Father which is in heaven.**
>
> Matt 18:19

> **Is any sick among you? let him call for the elders of the church; and let them pray over him, anointing him with oil in the name of the Lord:**
>
> James 5:14

> **And the prayer of faith shall save the sick, and the Lord shall raise him up; and if he have committed sins, they shall be forgiven him.**
>
> James 5:15

According to these verses it is alright to ask for others to pray for you, provided that they are in faith for your healing. Never ask someone to pray for you who does not believe the Word of God regarding healing. How can you agree with them?

However, having said this, if you are a strong Christian with absolute faith then you can receive healing yourself without anyone else. Sometimes it is good to get someone simply to agree with you in faith for your healing.

What about the anointing oil? Let us examine this from the Scriptures. The only references to oil in the New Testament linked with healing are James 5:14 and this verse from the Gospels:

> *And they cast out many devils, and anointed*
> *with oil many that were sick, and healed them.*
>
> Mark 6:13

When I was first in ministry over 20 years ago I was in a denomination that had a belief that oil should be used for praying for the sick. These verses seem to suggest this. However, I want you to read what I believe now about the use of oil. In the Old Testament the oil was a symbol of the Holy Spirit, like when Samuel anointed David with oil to be the next king:

> *And he sent, and brought him in. Now he*
> *was ruddy, and withal of a beautiful*
> *countenance, and goodly to look to. And the*
> *LORD said, Arise, anoint him: for this is he.*
>
> 1 Sam 16:12

> **Then Samuel took the horn of oil, and**
> **anointed him in the midst of his brethren:**
> **and the Spirit of the LORD came upon**
> **David from that day forward. So Samuel**
> **rose up, and went to Ramah.**
>
> 1 Sam 16:13

And so you have similar events throughout the Old Testament. Now, when Jesus came on the scene He prayed for sick people regularly and HE NEVER USED OIL AT ALL! However, He told His disciples to use oil in the above verse because they had not been filled with the Holy Spirit yet! After the Day of Pentecost the apostles prayed for the sick many times and NEVER USED OIL AT ALL.

You see, The Holy Spirit replaces the oil under the New Testament. The only other reference to oil is in James, which we have already quoted. I believe that this is simply a safeguard just in case the elders are not baptised in the Holy Spirit. If it was meant that we always used oil then Jesus would have done it and so would the apostles in the Acts. Once you are baptised in the Holy Spirit and speak with tongues then you can lay hands on the sick without oil and see results. Hallelujah! Anyway, if oil was essential to healing then you would have to carry it with you at all times, which would be ridiculous. Fancy saying to someone on a flight, 'I would love to pray for you but I left my oil in the baggage which is in the hold!'. You never know when you are going to have to pray for someone. Thank God it is the power of the Holy Spirit and faith in God's Word that brings healing – not some olive oil!

James says clearly that it is the 'Prayer of faith that saves the sick', save here means heal. Having said all that, if someone comes to you with a bottle of oil and asks you to pray for them what should you do? If it will help the faith of the person then you must use it. Otherwise, don't bother and trust the Holy Spirit and His wonderful gifts to manifest through you and then stand in faith for complete healing. That is the responsibility of those who are strong in faith.

CHAPTER 8   *Asking others to Pray for You*

CHAPTER 9

SPIRITS OF INFIRMITY

> And, behold, there was **a woman which had a spirit of infirmity eighteen years,** and was bowed together, and could in no wise lift up herself. And when Jesus saw her, he called her to him, and said unto her, 'Woman, thou art loosed from thine infirmity.' And he laid his hands on her: and immediately she was made straight and glorified God... 'And ought not this woman, being a daughter of Abraham, whom Satan hath bound, lo, these eighteen years, be loosed from this bond on the Sabbath day?'

> Luke 13:11 – 13,16

A spirit of infirmity usually causes a condition which cannot be diagnosed by the medical profession. The reason is because it is caused by a spirit which can often move around to different parts of the body. Many people who are prayed for to be healed of a spirit of infirmity can often feel it move, as they are prayed for, to a different part of the body. Also, when people pray generally for a person to be healed they often seem to get worse because their prayers have a provoking affect upon the spirit of infirmity, almost as if it has become angry; and so it causes much affliction.In the above story you will notice carefully that Jesus deals with the spirit of infirmity first and then He prays for healing for the woman. It is evident that the spirit of infirmity had actually caused this woman to be bent double and once the spirit of infirmity had been cast out she still needed physical healing from the damage left by the spirit. Thus it seems like Jesus is praying twice for her, but actually He is being very thorough, to help the precious lady to a complete healing.

*That it might be fulfilled which was spoken by Isaiah the prophet, saying, **Himself took our infirmities**, and bare our sicknesses.*

Matt 8:17

*But so much the more went there a fame abroad of him: and great multitudes came together to hear, and **to be healed by him of their infirmities.***

Luke 5:15

And in that same hour he cured many of their infirmities and plagues, and of evil spirits; and unto many that were blind he gave sight.

Luke 7:21

And certain women, which had been healed of evil spirits and infirmities, Mary called Magdalene, out of whom went seven devils,

Luke 8:2

I have ministered to many people who have had such a spirit of infirmity. I remember a lady who came for prayer one time who had not slept for weeks because of a pain in her knees.

As I went to pray for her, the Spirit of God spoke to me and said that it was a spirit of infirmity. So I cast out the spirit of infirmity and she fell fast under the power of God. She was in her 70's. She told me the next day that she had been completely healed and slept perfectly all night. Praise God!

I have known situations where a spirit of infirmity has affected all sorts of areas of the body; the heart, ears, eyes, knees, back, shoulders, lungs etc. Often they will simply leave as you rebuke them in the Name of Jesus Christ. However, there are some that you will need to name. There are two ways to get the name of a spirit like this. Firstly, ask the Lord for word of knowledge. Secondly I sometimes ask the spirit to name itself to me. It will reveal itself to the person and you simply ask the person what has come into their mind. I have found that it is always the first thing that enters their thought process. Once you have the name you can simply rebuke it and command it to go in The Mighty Name of Jesus Christ! I will then pray for healing for any damage caused by the spirit, just like Jesus did.

> And a certain man was there, **which had an infirmity thirty and eight years.**
>
> John 5:5

> When Jesus saw him lie, and knew that he had been now a long time in that case, he saith unto him, Wilt thou be made whole?
>
> John 5:6

> The impotent man answered him, Sir, I have no man, when the water is troubled, to put me into the pool: but while I am coming, another steppeth down before me.
>
> John 5:7

> **Jesus saith unto him, Rise, take up thy bed, and walk**.
>
> John 5:8

> *And immediately the man was made whole, and took up his bed, and walked: and on the same day was the sabbath.*
>
> John 5:9

This does not actually say that it was a spirit of infirmity but it would seem to suggest to me that it was, but Jesus dealt with it anyway! Don't get too caught up with always having to know what you are dealing with, because God makes up for our ignorance as we step out in faith.

If you suspect that your own situation may be caused by a spirit of infirmity then you can begin by taking authority against it yourself right now in Jesus' Name. Alternatively, you could ask your leaders to come and pray against it and then pray for your healing. Sometimes, fasting and prayer is needed before praying for someone so that we accurately discern its operation.

CHAPTER 10

SOME WONDERFUL
TESTIMONIES OF HEALING

During the years I have experienced some glorious miracles of healing myself, as well as hearing about them from other ministries. I would like to start by sharing one of the most powerful testimonies that I have ever heard which happened a few years ago through the ministry of the late Benson Idahosa.

Benson was visiting with the top government officials of his country and was in a block of offices several stories up. Apparently, one of the windows was open and an assistant official leaned against the window by accident, not realising that it was unlocked. While Benson was in conversation with the leaders this man fell out of the window and landed head first onto the concrete pavement. His head split open on impact and he was instantly killed. Everyone was in a state of shock. However, Benson made his way down the stairs and approached the dead man. He placed his hands around the remains of the shattered skull and commanded him to live in the Name of Jesus Christ! Benson said that the power of God knit the man's head back together in his hands and he was restored to life perfectly whole. This is very similar to a story in the Bible. I will let the Word of God speak for itself:

> And upon the first day of the week, when the disciples came together to break bread, Paul preached unto them, ready to depart on the morrow; and continued his speech until midnight. And there were many lights in the upper chamber, where they were gathered together. And there sat in a window a certain young man named Eutychus, being fallen

> *into a deep sleep: and as Paul was long
> preaching, he sunk down with sleep, and fell
> down from the third loft, and was taken up
> dead. And Paul went down, and fell on him,
> and embracing him said, 'Trouble not
> yourselves; for his life is in him.' When he
> therefore was come up again, and had
> broken bread, and eaten, and talked a long
> while, even till break of day, so he departed.
> And they brought the young man alive, and
> were not a little comforted.*
>
> Acts 20:7 – 12

Many years ago while I was pastoring a church in Salford, I had a word of knowledge about eleven people with varicose veins and that the Lord wanted to heal them. Seven people came forward. (I think that there were four stubborn people who did not want to come out).I prayed in obedience to God's word given to me and five of the people were instantly healed. The veins went back to normal before everyone's sight. Some were crying for joy. One lady who had very strong faith believed the word that was prayed and stood in faith. In the evening she testified that all her veins had been miraculously healed. The other lady who was in a backslidden state was never healed because her heart was not right with God.

On another Sunday morning our church was full of people and I was leading worship with my eyes shut. As I was worshipping I had a word of knowledge about someone in the meeting with quadriplegia. I did not think about what I was saying and asked the congregation if the person with quadriplegia would kindly put their hand up! (Of course they couldn't, since this is a very serious condition which means paralysis of both arms and legs. I did not think about it and continued worshipping. I then called the other leaders to pray for the sick and I still had my eyes shut. All of a sudden I opened my eyes and our leaders had gathered around a lady in a wheelchair. The Spirit of God spoke to me and told me that she was the lady. All eyes were on me to see what I would do. I had been coveting the gift of faith for many years and this was the first time this gift had operated in me. I walked up to her and asked her to hold my hand. I prayed a simple prayer and rebuked quadriplegia in Jesus' Name. I then gently lifted her up out of the chair and she stood up and walked slowly. The church erupted with excitement. I then ran her around the church and she was crying for joy. I held the microphone to her mouth and asked if she was saved. She said 'No'. I said, 'would you like to know Jesus Christ as your personal saviour?' She said, 'Yes please!'. She was saved straight away. Unknown to me she had been brought to our church by her mother, who was a spiritualist, and had been for many years. She had heard about the miracles happening in our church and so brought her daughter for prayer. On the first visit she was healed! Hallelujah! We had a small revival after that and saw many such things happen.

On another Sunday morning the Lord spoke to me about physical blindness. Two people were brought to the front. One was a 70 year old man and the other was a six year old who was partially blind. The man was totally blind. I prayed in simple faith according to the word of knowledge and the man's eyes opened straight away. His wife later bought me a plaque which reads, 'And my eyes have seen the king'. This sits in our lounge at home as a reminder of that day. The little girl could read the writing on the overhead projector straight away after prayer and continued to be made whole over time.

And when he was come into the house, the blind men came to him: and Jesus saith unto them, 'Believe ye that I am able to do this?' They said unto him, 'Yea, Lord.' Then touched he their eyes, saying, 'According to your faith be it unto you.' **And their eyes were opened;** *and Jesus straitly charged them, saying, 'See that no man know it.'*

Matt 9:28 – 30

Then was brought unto him one possessed with a devil, blind, and dumb: and he healed him, insomuch that the blind and dumb both spake and saw.

Matt 12:22

And the blind and the lame came to him in the temple; and he healed them.

Matt 21:14

And he took the blind man by the hand, and led him out of the town; and when he had spit on his eyes, and put his hands upon him, he asked him if he saw ought. And he looked up, and said, 'I see men as trees, walking.' After that he put his hands again upon his eyes, and made him look up; and he was restored, and saw every man clearly.

Mark 8:23

This last case is interesting because Jesus prayed twice for the man before the full healing manifested. Now don't build a doctrine around this verse, saying that we are to pray many times for the same thing. This case is the exception to the rule. Everywhere else Jesus only prayed once and people were healed. We should expect the same results as Jesus.

> *'Verily, verily, I say unto you, He that believeth on me, the works that I do shall he do also; and greater works than these shall he do; because I go unto my Father.* And whatsoever ye shall ask in my name, that will I do, that the Father may be glorified in the Son. If ye shall ask any thing in my name, I will do it.'
>
> John 14:12 – 14

> *He that saith he abideth in him ought himself also so to walk, even as he walked.*
>
> I John 2:6

> Herein is our love made perfect, that we may have boldness in the day of judgment: *because as he is, so are we in this world.*
>
> I John 4:17

No wonder the Bible says this:

> *'And these signs shall follow them that believe; In my name shall they cast out devils; they shall speak with new tongues;*

*they shall take up serpents, and if they drink any deadly thing, it shall not hurt them; **they shall lay hands on the sick, and they shall recover.'** So then after the Lord had spoken unto them, he was received up into heaven, and sat on the right hand of God. **And they went forth, and preached every where, the Lord working with them, and confirming the word with signs following. Amen.***

Mark 16:17 – 20

I have been believing these Scriptures for 22 years and standing on them until I see the same absolute miracle-working power as Jesus and His followers saw. The Lord has taught me step by step as I have launched out in faith and I am seeing a greater measure of healing all the time as I keep walking each step with Him.

One day our son David developed a lump in his neck. He was only about three years old. Ruth and I prayed in faith and rebuked the lump. We took him to the doctor who examined him and said that he would have to operate and remove it. However, we had to wait a few weeks before they could fit him in and during that time we kept rejoicing in faith for his complete healing. Nothing happened in the natural. I was not moved by things which do appear! 2 Cor 10:7. He was admitted to the hospital with Ruth for an afternoon operation. I was still praising God for the complete healing without the need of an operation. In the morning the doctor decided to check and make sure that the lump was still there. It was and so they prepared for an afternoon operation.

I was at home studying and believing God. Ruth telephoned me at about 2:10pm to ask me to come and fetch her and David and take them home. I said, 'Why what has happened?' She said that they were about to operate but could not find any trace of a lump at all! Glory to God; and there has never been a lump there since and he is now 22 years old.

CHAPTER 11

THREE LEVELS OF DIVINE HEALING

A few years ago I read about a man called John G. Lake, who was called of God to go to South Africa and start churches through a miracle ministry. He said something about healing that really helped me to walk in a higher dimension, both for my own health but also to see greater results when ministering to others. The 3 levels which I will discuss are

1. Divine healing for those who are sick.
2. Divine health to stay healthy.
3. Divine life.

Firstly, it is important to mention that WE GET WHAT WE BELIEVE FOR. Thus, if you are only believing for small things that is all you will get. You are limited by your faith. I thank God that our faith can grow so that we can receive greater and greater things from God as we develop.

> *For therein is the righteousness of God revealed from faith to faith: as it is written, the just shall live by faith.*
>
> Rom 1:17

> *We are bound to thank God always for you, brethren, as it is meet, because that **your faith groweth exceedingly**, and the charity of every one of you all toward each other aboundeth;*
>
> II Th 1:3

Don't limit God by unbelief!

> *Yea, they turned back and tempted God, and limited the Holy One of Israel.*
>
> Ps 78:41

Wherever you are at in your faith for healing walk, I trust that the following will help many of you to reach much greater heights.

Firstly, Divine healing is available to those who are sick. There are many people who believe this and wait until they are ill before releasing any faith in the Word of God. I call this having your back up against the wall. Many people only have this revelation and so they get sick regularly, because their belief is, 'Every time I get sick I can claim Divine healing for my body'. Now it sounds good but there is something lacking here that needs to be addressed.

We have already shown that Jesus bore our sickness and carried our disease on the cross two thousand years ago, along with our sins. Now, you know that you are forgiven of all your sins and if you sin you know that you have forgiveness, because Jesus took all your sins on His body all those years ago. Thus, constant forgiveness is available to all of us who truly repent. Thank God for His mercy.

So it is with sickness and disease. The price has already been paid! Jesus has already done all He is going to about all our aches, pains, sickness, lumps etc. What we have to do is not to believe 'that I will get sick', but 'I am healed by His stripes'.

I was healed two thousand years ago and so my duty is to confess God's Word and be in agreement with Him, which stops the devil from having a chance to attack me. You see, FAITH IS SPOKEN.Study these verses carefully if you have not heard these things before:

> **We having the same spirit of faith, according as it is written, I believed, and therefore have I spoken; we also believe, and therefore speak;**
>
> 2 Cor 4:13

> *And Jesus answering saith unto them, 'Have faith in God. For verily I say unto you,* **That whosoever shall say unto this mountain, "Be thou removed, and be thou cast into the sea," and shall not doubt in his heart, but shall believe that those things which he saith shall come to pass; he shall have whatsoever he saith. Therefore I say unto you, What things soever ye desire, when ye pray, believe that ye receive them, and ye shall have them.'**
>
> Mark 11:22 – 24

Once I had understood this for myself I stopped believing and confessing that I get sick and started to say, *'thank you Lord that I am in health and that my body does not get sick in the name of Jesus Christ!'*

I have been doing this now for 22 years and it is only very occasionally that I have to resist sickness and disease but it goes in Jesus' Name. My responsibility is to keep speaking The Word of God and stay healthy. This is Divine Health which says that, since Jesus has already taken all my sickness and disease, I don't have to have any of it; and so I choose by faith to walk in Divine Health all the days of my life.

Here is a little confession that I confess regularly;

Christ has redeemed me from the curse of the law. Therefore, I forbid any sickness or disease to touch my body. Every disease, germ and every virus that comes near my body dies instantly in the name of Jesus Christ. Every organ and tissue of my body functions in the perfection to which God intended it to function and I forbid any malfunction in the name of Jesus Christ. I am healed and am going to stay that way!

This is walking in Divine health. Watch what you say about you! Never say, 'I am catching a cold', rather say, 'I am refusing a cold in Jesus Name'. 'A cold does not belong to me'. The same applies to cancer, arthritis and everything. Praise God.

There was once a man who wanted to go to America many years ago. He bought his ticket and sailed from Southampton to New York. The journey took many days. He took with him a bag containing lots of wafers and cheese portions for the journey. Each day when each meal was announced he would go into a little corner and eat some cheese and wafers and drink a little water. People looked at him as they went for their sumptuous food in the dining room. This continued each day until they were almost in New York, when one of the waiters came up to the man and asked him why he did not join the three meals a day. The man said that he had bought the ticket but did not have any money for the food. The waiter replied and told him the amazing truth. 'The food was all included in your ticket sir; you could have dined with us every day instead of eating those now mouldy wafers and smelly cheese!'I am sure that you are probably saying to yourself, 'What a silly man'. However, it is like many of us in the Christian life. Everything is included in the ticket! The day you were 'born again' you were saved for eternity, healed for life and delivered from poverty. However, you have to receive these things for yourself by faith and walk in it day by day. What do you want; three lovely meals in the dining hall or mouldy wafers and rotten cheese sitting in a corner by yourself? The choice is entirely yours. I know what I have chosen!

> *My people are destroyed for lack of knowledge:* *because thou hast rejected knowledge, I will also reject thee, that thou shalt be no priest to me: seeing thou hast forgotten the law of thy God, I will also forget thy children.*
>
> Hosea 4:6

> *According as his divine power hath given unto us all things that pertain unto life and godliness, through the knowledge of him that hath called us to glory and virtue:*
>
> 2 Pet 1:3

Simply receive your health right now and part company with all your infirmities and give them back to the devil who gave them to you!

CHAPTER 11   *Three levels of Divine Healing*

Now the third revelation takes us even further!

It is called Divine Life. This means that we are walking in Divine Health to such a degree that the healing power of God is flowing out of us all the time, so that any sick person that comes our way will be healed simply by being close to us. So it is not us who get sick but the sick person who gets healed!

Take a look at these verses!

> And there was in their synagogue a man with an unclean spirit; and he cried out, saying, **'Let us alone; what have we to do with thee, thou Jesus of Nazareth? art thou come to destroy us? I know thee who thou art, the Holy One of God.'** And Jesus rebuked him, saying, Hold thy peace, and come out of him. And when the unclean spirit had torn him, and cried with a loud voice, he came out of him. And they were all amazed insomuch that they questioned among themselves saying, 'What thing is this? What new doctrine is this? For with authority commandeth he even the unclean spirits, and they do obey him.' **...But Simon's wife's mother lay sick of a fever, and anon they tell him of her. And he came and took her by the hand, and lifted her up; and immediately the fever left her, and she ministered unto them.** And at even, when the sun did set, they brought

unto him all that were diseased, and them that were possessed with devils. And all the city was gathered together at the door.

Mark 1:23 – 27; 30 – 34

And he healed many that were sick of divers diseases, and cast out many devils; and suffered not the devils to speak, because they knew him.

Mark 1:34

Insomuch that they brought forth the sick into the streets, and laid them on beds and couches, that at the least the shadow of Peter passing by might overshadow some of them. There came also a multitude out of the cities round about unto Jerusalem, bringing sick folks, and them which were vexed with unclean spirits: and they were healed every one.

Acts 5:15 – 16

Thus, when sickness and disease comes near to a child of God walking in his covenant, the healing power of God emanates from us to heal the sick people. I have seen this in a measure from time to time and keep believing for it to become a regular trend. I was in India and had to preach to 2500 people. 358 people accepted Jesus Christ to be their saviour. I asked them to put their hands down again and explained the Gospel again and the same 358 hands went up. I had a team that did the oounting! After they had been led to Christ I was then led by the Holy Spirit to minister healing but not by the laying on of hands. I simply prayed from the front and the healing power of God touched about 1500 people. The people were testifying to being healed for four hours after the service had finished!

We have had people who came to our church and came into the meeting sick and were healed simply by being in a place of Divine Health. Whatever place you are at right now in your faith for healing why not spend some time now in prayer and read through this chapter a few times and receive the highest revelation of all? He has healed you by His stripes. Healing is flowing from you to others. Believe it right now and speak it forth.

CHAPTER 12

ALL KINDS OF HEALING

Take a look at these Scriptures:

> *And Jesus went about all Galilee, teaching in their synagogues,* **and preaching the gospel of the kingdom, and healing all manner of sickness and all manner of disease among the people.** *And his fame went throughout all Syria: and* **they brought unto him all sick people that were taken with divers diseases and torments, and those which were possessed with devils, and those which were lunatick, and those that had the palsy; and he healed them.**
>
> Matt 4:23 – 24

These verses alone cover virtually all kinds of suffering that we come across still today. Thus, your healing, health and wholeness has been paid for completely. This includes all emotional problems, all relationship breakdowns, nervous and mental breakdowns, all mental problems, including insanity. It includes healing from all sexual problems – physical, mental and emotional. You can be a virgin again in Christ Jesus. The Lord can heal your memory so that you are as pure as the driven snow.

Healing has already been paid for all A.I.D.S. sufferers and all kinds of sexually transmitted diseases. I know a preacher in Florida who had the full H.I.V. virus and was given months to live. Jesus healed him completely when he cried out to God in full repentance. He now goes around youth groups and has a growing ministry to help to bring health and healthy living to the youth of his area.

Of course, the best way is not to get involved with anyone sexually, apart from in the God-ordained manner of marriage. All deviations from the truth of God's word is thin ice. Homosexuality and lesbianism are not Christian practices and will be judged accordingly. Read about Sodom in the book of Genesis if you don't believe me.

Let us look now at abortion. Can God heal you if you have had an abortion? Firstly, you need to repent of murder. From the moment of conception you have produced life. Repent and receive mercy right now and God will forgive you. Then receive healing from guilt, torment etc. If you were raped then you need to forgive the man who raped you, right now. Healing is yours and has been paid for.

I was in a meeting years ago and was preaching on healing. Many people came forward for healing. I had prayed for about 150 people and had to catch a flight the next morning very early. The service went on until about 11:00 at night. There were about 5 people left in the building and I was ready for bed! A young lady was sobbing at the back of the church. She would not speak to anyone; she just cried. We knew that something was wrong. The youth leader spoke to her and found out that on her 18th. birthday she had been raped on her way home. She had told nobody about it. She was now 21 and could not look at a man, let alone touch one. I was asked to minister to her at 12:00 midnight. I told her that she needed to forgive him. She prayed the prayer and I rebuked the spirit of rape and guilt from off her. She was immediately free. She jumped up and threw her arm around me. I knew that she was free to be able to do that! Praise God. So, how important is forgiveness then?

Let us look at some Scriptures;

> *And forgive us our debts, as* **we forgive our debtors.**
> Matt 6:12

> **For if ye forgive men their trespasses, your heavenly Father will also forgive you: but if ye forgive not men their trespasses, neither will your Father forgive your trespasses.**
> Matt 6:14 – 15

> **Then came Peter to him, and said, 'Lord, how oft shall my brother sin against me, and I forgive him? Till seven times?' Jesus saith unto him, 'I say not unto thee, Until seven times: but, Until seventy times seven.'**
> Matt 18:21 – 22

> **So likewise shall my heavenly Father do also unto you, if ye from your hearts forgive not every one his brother their trespasses.**
> Matt 18:35

> **And when ye stand praying, forgive, if ye have ought against any: that your Father also which is in heaven may forgive you your trespasses. But if ye do not forgive, neither will your Father which is in heaven forgive your trespasses.**
> Mark 11:25 – 26

I have pastored hundreds of people over 20 years and I have had to talk to so many people about the area of forgiveness. I have had to forgive people many times also. In fact, in pastoring, I regularly forgive people over and over again. In fact I feel like saying, 'I forgive this sister even before she says anything to me to save time later'. It seems that all of us have to walk in forgiveness. It is the love walk. I had something that happened to me a few years ago that stretched me so much in the area of forgiveness. We were holding a healing service in our church and a man walked into our church and joined the healing line. I prayed for him along with all the others. He left the meeting before it had finished and went into the office section of our buildings. He went into my office (which is now kept locked at all times) and stole my lap top computer, cd player etc and walked out of the church. I went into my office and had my usual cup of coffee. I noticed that all my equipment had gone. I was just coming off the mountain top from ministering and was not ready to deal with such a situation. I was really angry and hurt. My wife came into my room and was angry too. The Lord spoke to me and simply said, 'Rejoice'. I felt like finding the man and thumping him and then asking for forgiveness later. That is how I felt. I prayed and asked the Lord why this had happened. The Lord said that the devil hated my books and wanted to slow them down. The Lord also said to me that my laptop was now 18 months old and God wanted me to have a new one! I forgave the man straight away after hearing that and went about my business. 21 days later a man came up to me and bought me a brand new state of the art lap top and I have had a new one every 18 months ever since; all because of forgiveness! If I had not forgiven him then I would probably be in a real mess now and certainly would not have a new laptop. We all have to walk in forgiveness! In fact, every time the devil has stolen something from me God has turned it around for me and I have ended up with something far better! Hallelujah!

A prophet came up to me one time in India and said that he had a word from God for me. He prophesied over me that great things would happen in my life and ministry, simply because I walked in forgiveness. I believe that word and expect that one day God will use me in a bigger way for His eternal Glory! My attitude is that I am just getting started and keep walking humbly with God every day and just take each step that He gives me.

What has all this got to do with healing? Everything! Unforgiveness stops all the promises of God working for you! As soon as you forgive then all the things that God says are available for you.

If you have any of the following in your life then it began with unforgiveness;

Resentment, Bitterness, Hate, Anger, Thoughts of murder etc.

These are very serious conditions and need to be addressed right now. Start by forgiving that person or persons that caused these reactions in you. Then renounce each one; 'I renounce all resentment from my life in the name of Jesus Christ!' Then do it with all these negative, destructive emotions. This is real inner healing! Freedom will come to you as you forgive *from your heart*. You say, "I have tried that many times". Well, start believing that God has forgiven you by faith. You may have to forgive someone a few times as the layers are peeled off you. It is a bit like an onion. You peel one layer off and then another comes. That is how the devil builds a stronghold against you. It can be prevented by forgiving all through life, but if you have let it in then *there is still full healing for you!* Praise God!

I have been in healing lines and prayed for someone who was sick. The Spirit of God has spoken to me many times and said simply, 'They need to forgive'. I will ask the person to forgive and after they have forgiveness I hardly have to pray for them. Healing is often instantaneous after the person has forgiven.

I have had a few who say they have forgiven and I pray for them and I know in my heart that they have not. I have sometimes challenged people and some have even shouted at me and said, 'I have forgiven them'. Then, while under the ministry of the Holy Spirit, that same person has said, 'I hate him, I hate him'. Hatred was buried deep in the heart and The Holy Spirit searched it out. Forgiveness comes and the person is completely healed of all hate, anger etc. Sometimes we need to dig a bit deeper.

> *Let all bitterness, and wrath, and anger, and clamour, and evil speaking, be put away from you, with all malice:*
> Eph 4:31

Looking diligently lest any man fail of the grace of God; **lest any root of bitterness springing up trouble you, and thereby many be defiled;**

Heb 12:15

Another real enemy is a thing called UNBELIEF.

And he did not many mighty works there because of their unbelief.

Matt 13:58

And he marvelled because of their unbelief. And he went round about the villages, teaching.

Mark 6:6

Afterward he appeared unto the eleven as they sat at meat, and upbraided them with their unbelief and hardness of heart, because they believed not them which had seen him after he was risen.

Mark 16:14

He staggered not at the promise of God through unbelief; but was strong in faith, giving glory to God;

Rom 4:20

Take heed, brethren, lest there be in any of you an evil heart of unbelief, in departing from the living God.

Heb 3:12

So we see that they could not enter in because of unbelief.

Heb 3:19

Let us labour therefore to enter into that rest, lest any man fall after the same example of unbelief.

Heb 4:11

Unfortunately, the devil knows these Scriptures and uses unbelief against all of us at times to rob us of the blessings of God. I like what a man by the name of Lester Sumrall said;

'feed your faith and starve your doubt to death'.

In other words, don't give unbelief a chance in your life. It works in the same way that unforgiveness works. We have to repent of it before it takes root. If you have any thoughts in you of unbelief then take all those thoughts captive and rebuke them and forbid them from having any place in you.

Casting down imaginations, and every high thing that exalteth itself against the knowledge of God, and bringing into captivity every thought to the obedience of Christ;

2 Cor 10:5

Unbelief is one of the things that you will have to fight if you have been brought up in an environment of unbelief, religion etc; even if it was a born again upbringing! Some people have a revelation of salvation but are opposed to healing and any other aspect of our covenant in Christ Jesus.

> ***And be not conformed to this world: but be ye transformed by the renewing of your mind, that ye may prove what is that good, and acceptable, and perfect, will of God.***
>
> Rom 12:2

We need our mind washing with the water of the Word every day so that faith can come and healing can be a reality.

> *Therefore it is of faith, that it might be by grace; to the end the promise might be sure to all the seed; not to that only which is of the law, but to that also which is of the faith of Abraham; who is the father of us all, (As it is written, I have made thee a father of many nations,) before him whom he believed, even God, who quickeneth the dead, and calleth those things which be not as though they were.* **Who against hope believed in hope**, *that he might become the father of many nations; according to that which was spoken, So shall thy seed be.* **And being not weak in faith, he considered not his own body now dead, when he was about an hundred years old, neither yet the deadness of Sarah's womb: He staggered not at the promise of God through unbelief; but was strong in faith, giving**

glory to God; And being fully persuaded that, what he had promised, he was able also to perform.

Rom 4:16 – 21

So then faith cometh by hearing, and hearing by the word of God.

Rom 10:17

For I say, through the grace given unto me, to every man that is among you, not to think of himself more highly than he ought to think; but to think soberly, according as God hath dealt to every man the measure of faith.

Rom 12:3

For we walk by faith, not by sight:

2 Cor 5:7

Now the just shall live by faith: but if any man draw back, my soul shall have no pleasure in him.

Heb 10:38

Now faith is the substance of things hoped for, the evidence of things not seen.

Heb 11:1

But without faith it is impossible to please him: for he that cometh to God must believe that he is, and that he is a rewarder of them that diligently seek him.

Heb 11:6

Let me tell you about Abraham. His faith just kept on growing even after Isaac was born. Did you know that after Sarah had died Abraham went on to marry again and have 6 more children? See Gen 25:1. The name of Abraham's new wife was Keturah.

Faith is strong stuff! He went on to live until he was 175 years old! No wonder the devil fights faith so much. Don't ever criticise someone who is walking by faith. Even when we get things wrong the Lord will be there to add the finishing touches to our efforts of faith and get us through!

> *Looking unto Jesus the author and finisher of our faith; who for the joy that was set before him endured the cross, despising the shame, and is set down at the right hand of the throne of God.*
>
> Heb 12:2

Keep strong in faith all the days of your life and don't leave room for unbelief to creep back in again! Take authority against it and treat it as the worst kind of enemy.

CHAPTER 13

BREAKING BREAD CORRECTLY

For I have received of the Lord that which also I delivered unto you, That the Lord Jesus the same night in which he was betrayed took bread: And when he had given thanks, he broke it, and said, 'Take, eat: this is my body, which is broken for you: **this do in remembrance of me.'** *After the same manner also he took the cup, when he had supped, saying, 'This cup is the new testament in my blood: this do ye, as oft as ye drink it, in remembrance of me.' For as often as ye eat this bread, and drink this cup, ye do shew the Lord's death till he come.* **Wherefore whosoever shall eat this bread, and drink this cup of the Lord, unworthily, shall be guilty of the body and blood of the Lord. But let a man examine himself, and so let him eat of that bread, and drink of that cup. For he that eateth and drinketh unworthily, eateth and drinketh damnation to himself, not discerning the Lord's body. For this cause many are weak and sickly among you, and many sleep.** *For if we would judge ourselves, we should not be judged. But when we are judged, we are chastened of the Lord, that we should not be condemned with the world.*

1 Cor 11:23

Verse 30 says 'many sleep'. This really means; to put to sleep, decease or to be dead. This puts a very serious aspect on how we break bread! We need to discern the Lord's body properly. This means many things. That is why we are to examine ourselves first.

Wo nood to chcck that we are walking in forgiveness and love to all our fellow believers. We must make sure that we are right with our wife or husband! Also, we need to be properly submitted to our leaders! I recently had a situation where someone in our church was not getting better from quite a serious illness. It transpired that he was never in true submission to me as the pastor. My prayers for him have not been working, since he was walking In rebellion. I pray that he repents. It is so important that each of us is submitted to those in leadership over us. Look at these Scriptures!

> *And we beseech you, brethren, to know them which labour among you, and are over you in the Lord, and admonish you; And to esteem them very highly in love for their work's sake. And be at peace among yourselves.*
>
> 1Thes 5:12

> *Obey them that have the rule over you, and submit yourselves: for they watch for your souls, as they that must give account, that they may do it with joy, and not with grief: for that is unprofitable for you.*
>
> Heb 13:17

That says to me that I have to give an account for all the sheep I have ever pastored. Also, the account that I give will affect their reward in eternity! Unfortunately, I will not be able to give a very good account of some people, but I will have to speak the truth on that day! Repent now of anything you have said about those who lead you. It will affect your health! That is why we should examine ourselves first before we break bread and take of the cup.

CHAPTER

CHAPTER 14

HEALING FROM A POOR SELF IMAGE

You may already identify with this title or you may understand the terms insecurity or inferiority. Many people suffer from such things, mainly because of their upbringing or church background. My wife Ruth had a crushed spirit from childhood, which prevented her from being able to make decisions or even speak to anyone. Ruth had a poor self image when I married her but thought that she was just quiet and shy. We would sit in a room together and I would talk away and Ruth would nod her head or just give yes or no answers. Many years later she admitted to me that she did not feel that her words meant anything to anybody else. This is a poor self image. It produces no confidence at all and affects our whole life. It is difficult to get a good job with a poor self image etc. Thus, a poor self image will affect our destiny and our wealth.

However, Ruth is totally different these days! She is a preacher and Bible teacher and is now a pastor in her own right! She has been healed of a poor self image. She no longer feels inferior and she is good at making decisions. It did not happen overnight. Ruth came to me one day and asked me if I thought that she needed any deliverence from these things. I said I didn't think so, in my ignorance. I prayed for her and she started to manifest all kinds of things.

After many sessions of prayer for healing and deliverance Ruth is a different person. She has also found out who she is in Christ Jesus by revelation, instead of just having the head knowledge. It is one thing to know something in your mind but another to have it in your heart. We call this 'revelation knowledge'.

CHAPTER 14   *Healing from a Poor Self Image*

The wicked flee when no man pursueth:
but the righteous are bold as a lion.

Prov 28:1

We are what the Word of God says we are but we have to believe it. A poor self image will rob you of all of this. Thus we need healing from it. This happens by meditating on the Word of God and confessing it. This brings a measure of healing. As thoughts of a poor self image arise in your heart then rebuke them in Jesus Name. You may need deliverance from such things, also by someone who knows about this ministry. Here are a few Scriptures for you to start with:

And the LORD shall make thee the head, and not the tail; and thou shalt be above only, and thou shalt not be beneath; if that thou hearken unto the commandments of the LORD thy God, which I command thee this day, to observe and to do them:

Deut 28:13

And hath made us kings and priests unto God and his Father; to him be glory and dominion for ever and ever. Amen.

Rev 1:6

Little children, let no man deceive you: he that doeth righteousness is righteous, even as he is righteous.

I Jn 3:7

Herein is our love made perfect, that we may have boldness in the day of judgment: because as he is, so are we in this world.

I Jn 4:17

The Power of Love!

Love is the best healer of all! We need to love ourselves because we are made in His image. If we hate ourselves (I don't mean our flesh life; that we must hate!) then we hate God who made us. We are special, precious, unique etc. If God loves us then we ought to love ourselves.

Honour thy father and thy mother: and, Thou shalt love thy neighbour as thyself.

Matt 19:19

How can you love others if you hate yourself? That is why you cannot make relationships very well. Self hatred will manifest itself through you to others without you realising it. Make a decision today to love you. Look in the mirror and say to yourself, 'I accept me as I am and I love the person that God made me so that I can become the best me that I can for His Glory!' For some of you that will be the most significant healing of all!

You will never be anybody else so you might as well get on with you since you have to live with yourself until Jesus comes back. I am convinced that a person will never fulfil their personal destiny while they hate themselves.

Also, we are to love God and seek to serve Him to the best of our abilities. Don't put yourself under condemnation by trying to be what you are not. Do what God called you to do and you will be fulfilled all the days of your life. To love God is to obey Him. That will bring all kinds of healing to you!

> *If ye keep my commandments, ye shall abide in my love; even as I have kept my Father's commandments, and abide in his love.*
>
> John 15:10

> *By this we know that we love the children of God, when we love God, and keep his commandments. For this is the love of God, that we keep his commandments: and his commandments are not grievous.*
>
> I Jn 5:2 – 3

Love has the ability to soften the hardest heart and bring all kinds of healing inside. The love of God heals the broken hearted and melts away the pain of a broken relationship. The love of God sets us free from grief, even when we lose a loved one. You see we need to be healed from all of these things so that we can find our purpose again and do something useful with our lives, instead of sitting around and feeling sorry for ourselves!

> *Finally, brethren, farewell. Be perfect, be of good comfort, be of one mind, live in peace, and the God of love and peace shall be with you.*
>
> 2 Cor 13:11

The grace of the Lord Jesus Christ, and the love of God, and the communion of the Holy Ghost, be with you all. Amen.

2 Cor 13:14

*For in Jesus Christ neither circumcision availeth any thing, nor uncircumcision; **but faith which worketh by love.***

Gal 5:6

For, brethren, ye have been called unto liberty; only use not liberty for an occasion to the flesh, but by love serve one another.

Gal 5:13

But the fruit of the Spirit is love, joy, peace, longsuffering, gentleness, goodness, faith,

Gal 5:22

But God, who is rich in mercy, for his great love wherewith he loved us,

Eph 2:4

That Christ may dwell in your hearts by faith; that ye, being rooted and grounded in love,

Eph 3:17

And to know the love of Christ, which passeth knowledge, that ye might be filled with all the fulness of God.

Eph 3:19

And walk in love, as Christ also hath loved us, and hath given himself for us an offering and a sacrifice to God for a sweetsmelling savour.

Eph 5:2

*Charity suffereth long, and is kind; charity envieth not; charity vaunteth not itself, is not puffed up, doth not behave itself unseemly, seeketh not her own, is not easily provoked, thinketh no evil; rejoiceth not in iniquity, but rejoiceth in the truth; beareth all things, believeth all things, hopeth all things, endureth all things. **Charity never faileth: but whether there be prophecies, they shall fail; whether there be tongues, they shall cease; whether there be knowledge, it shall vanish away.***

1 Cor 13:4 – 8

Love never fails! Hallelujah!

We all need a fresh revelation of love into our hearts so that we can walk in constant healing and wholeness, inside and out!

CHAPTER 15

HEREDITARY AND ANCESTRAL CURSES

Many people that I have met who have had problems with their health that could not be easily identified have often needed prayer to be freed from a generational curse. These are curses that are passed down from our ancestors etc.

One of the very common curses comes from freemasonry. This evil practice causes all sorts of major problems in children and grandchildren, since it is direct Satan worship. Until a freemason reaches the 33rd. degree he is not told that the god who he has been bowing down to is called Lucifer. The children of masons often suffer terrible illnesses etc. I was once asked to go and pray for a man who had a chronic ailment which was killing him. I went into his house after driving 200 miles and we sat down and talked. The man wanted me to pray for him for healing. The Spirit of God stopped me just before I was about to pray and said to me, 'This man is a freemason'. I asked him and he very reluctantly admitted it. I told him that he needed to renounce freemasonry completely and God would heal him. I tried everything to help him to see but he would not. I then told him that I could not pray for him because my prayers would be useless. He had been born again but would not renounce this evil practice.In my own life I used to suffer with hay fever, which is a horrible condition. I did everything I knew in faith to get victory over it. I had gained about 30 percent but knew that there must be something else. I went to be prayed for by a well known preacher with a strong healing ministry and he had a word from God for me that it was due to a curse through my mother. I believed it and rebuked it. I have been healed ever since! This is where we need to open to the gifts of the Holy Spirit and also where we need each other from time to time. If you know that you have a condition that you have stood in faith against, then keep standing but also ask the Holy Spirit if anything is hindering the full manifestation of healing. Listen to what God says to you and then act on it. Ask your pastors to pray for you also, since they are your spiritual covering. God can use them through the gifts of the Spirit to help you.

We all need the Spiritual Gifts from time to time:

> But the manifestation of the Spirit is given to every man to profit withal. **For to one is given by the Spirit the word of wisdom; to another the word of knowledge by the same Spirit; to another faith by the same Spirit; to another the gifts of healing by the same Spirit; to another the working of miracles;** to another prophecy; **to another discerning of spirits;** to another divers kinds of tongues; to another the interpretation of tongues: but all these worketh that one and the selfsame Spirit, dividing to every man severally as he will.
>
> 1 Cor 12:7

All the gifts that I have highlighted in bold are used for healing. The Bible tells us that we are to covet these gifts to help each other. The Lord gives these giftings to help to bring healing to the body. Ask that you might be used in them today. I need these gifts all the time! Thus we can stand on the Word of God but also allow the gifts of the Spirit to be used to show us anything that would stop a full manifestation of healing in us or those we are ministering to.

The Lord has graciously sent me all over the world and I regularly sense the anointing for healing and miracles coming upon me. Sometimes I teach the body of Christ what the Word says and sometimes The Holy Spirit does a mighty work. We need both the Word and The Spirit to be fully mature in this area of healing.

I want to finish with a wonderful testimony of healing that happened a few years ago in Australia.

I was speaking at a large church in one of the main cities in 'Ossie'. It was a Sunday night and I was led to preach on healing, deliverance and miracles etc. Now, I had met the pastor before a couple of times and had noticed that he was very much overweight. However, he was now much slimmer. The last time I saw him he was much larger and his knees were giving way under the weight of his body. He had decided that he was going to lose this weight. He went on a very strict diet for one whole year, of just having fresh fruit for breakfast each morning from Monday till Friday and then eating normally at the weekend. He lost all that weight but his knees were still giving him a lot of trouble. He could not walk properly, even after losing all of that weight. However, he was standing in faith on God's Word for his complete healing and wholeness. On the Sunday evening I gave the appeal for anyone to come forward for healing, and he was the first to come out along with about a hundred others. I prayed a simple prayer over him and then went to the next person. I did not see him again until the Wednesday morning for another healing service. He got up and told us all what had happened since I had prayed for him. On the Monday morning he tried to get out of bed but was in much pain in his knees and it did not look like anything had happened. He kept confessing God's Word for healing and agreeing with God and His Word. On the Monday night he was worse than ever. On the Tuesday morning he arose from his bed and his knees were in tormenting pain. I had to preach after this testimony and wanted to get on the next flight out of there at this point! He then said that on the Tuesday evening something popped in both his knees and he was completely healed. He showed us his knees and he was jumping for joy! Hallelujah! Don't give up until the full manifestation of healing comes!

> ***Beloved, I wish above all things that thou mayest prosper and be in health, even as thy soul prospereth.***
>
> 3 Jn 1:2

Enjoy your healing, stay healthy, eat the right food, do some exercise, speak the Word of Faith, forgive everyone and keep seeking His face.

Time!

Finally, I want to say something that may seem obvious to many but affects us all.

Some things take time to heal! The loss of a loved one for instance, usually takes time to heal from the emotional upheaval and shock. We can take authority against the spirit of grief but it still takes time to get over the void of someone that we have loved for so long.

I think that we have all had situations in our lives that have taken their toll on us, whether we admit to it or not! I am no exception. There have been things in my life that have taken years to get over and some things a few weeks or months. However, I thank God that we can be healed completely, even if it takes some time. This is where patience is needed.

OTHER BOOKS BY
TREVOR NEWPORT

What the Bible says about YOUR Provision
and Prosperity

Did you go OR were you sent? (An Autobiography)

King Jesus is Coming Soon!

Angels, Demons and Spiritual Warfare

The Ministry of Jesus Christ

Divine Appointments

The Two U's: Unbelief and Unforgiveness

Secrets of Success

From Victory to Victory

Pitfalls in Ministry

How to Pray in the Spirit

The Anointing: the Vital Ingredient

A Practical Guide to Fasting

Prophets, Prophesying and Personal Prophecy

Absolute Faith

As Jesus Is, So Are We in This World

Sharpening Iron: Developing Godly Relationships